AF428384

CAN SURFERS SURF ON TSUNAMIS?

ENVIRONMENT BOOKS FOR KIDS

Children's Environment Books

Speedy Publishing LLC

40 E. Main St. #1156

Newark, DE 19711

www.speedypublishing.com

n this book, we're going to talk about the deadly waves called tsunamis. So, let's get right to it!

Surfer at the bottom of a huge crashing wave.

WHAT IS A TSUNAMI?

The word *"Tsunami"* translates to *"Harbor Wave"* in the Japanese language. Tsunamis are waves, but they're not ordinary waves. Instead of dissipating as they reach the shoreline, they increase in size as they approach the shore. As they hit the land, they cause an incredible amount of destruction.

The wall of water from a tsunami travels at a speed that is as fast as a jet, up to 500 miles per hour. As it hits the shore, it begins to slow down, but it grows in height. Everything in its path is demolished and many people die as they are swept out in the waves.

Surreal image of huge waves surrounding dry sand.

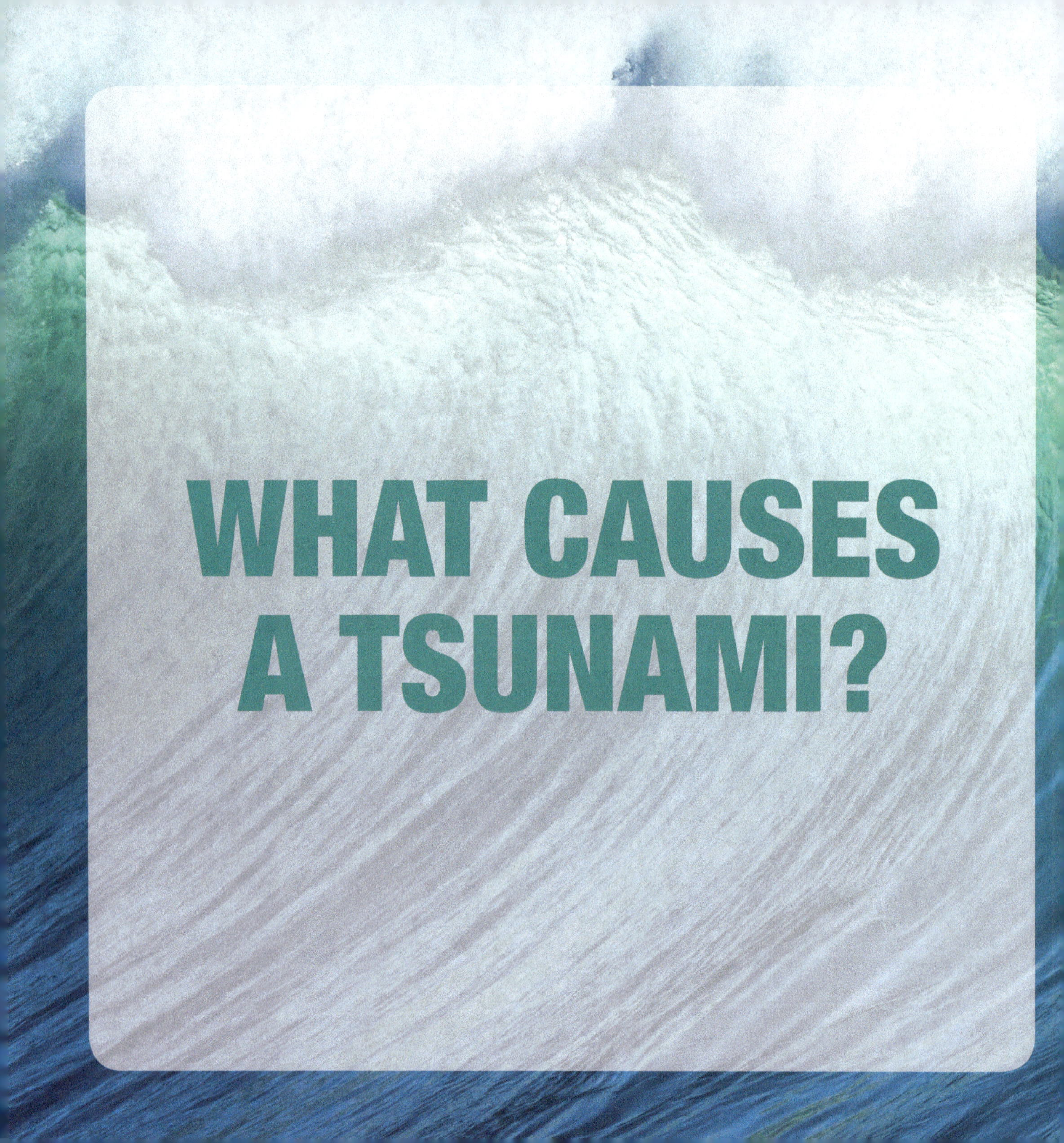

WHAT CAUSES A TSUNAMI?

A tsunami is caused by a very large amount of water being displaced. Tsunamis are created by major geological events. Powerful earthquakes and volcanic eruptions can cause them. Massive landslides and huge chunks breaking off from glaciers can trigger tsunamis as well.

Earthquakes are usually the cause of tsunamis. When the Earth's tectonic plates shift underwater, it causes a gap where none was there before. As the ocean water fills this gap, the displacement of water causes the tsunami to begin. Think about what happens if you're taking a bath and you suddenly jerk forward and back.

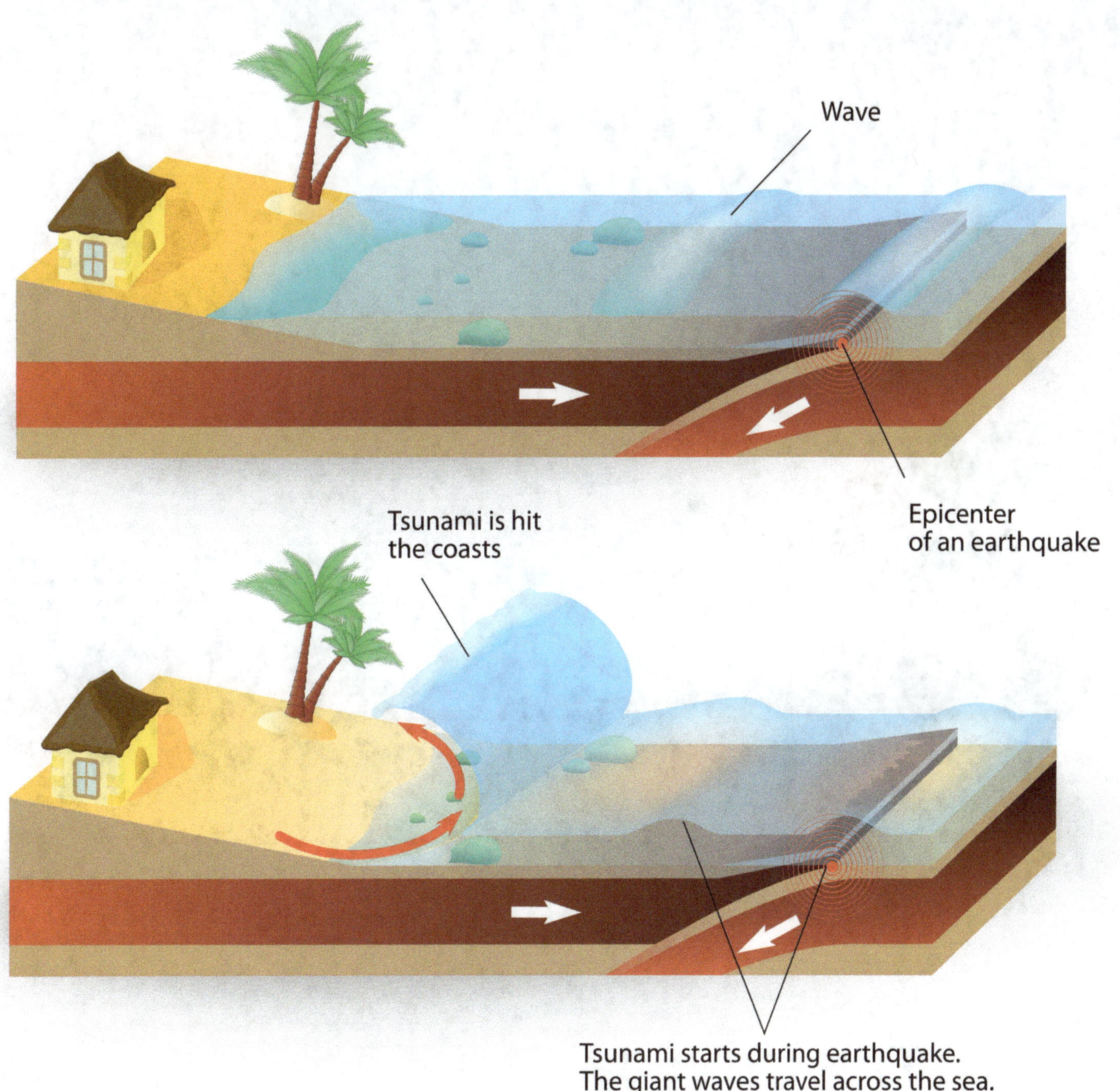

Wave
Epicenter
of an earthquake
Tsunami is hit
the coasts
Tsunami starts during earthquake.
The giant waves travel across the sea.

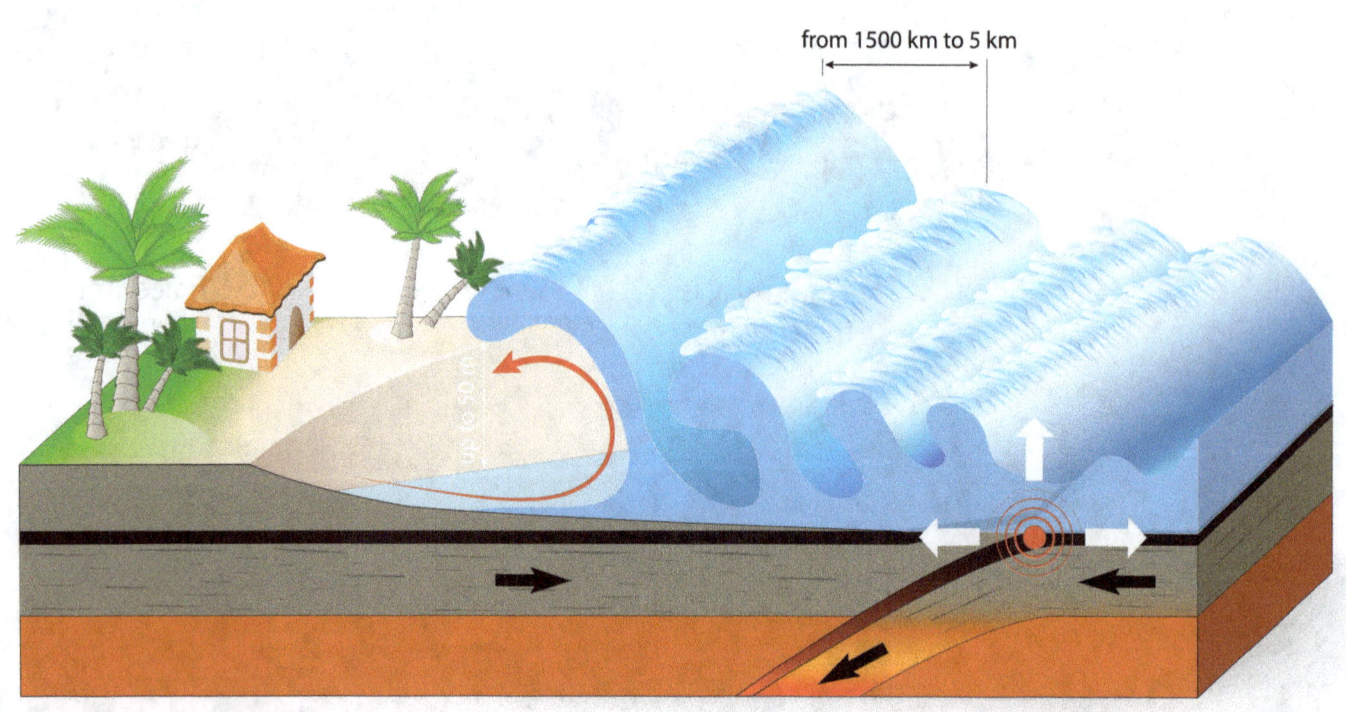

from 1500 km to 5 km

A s your body moves, the displacement of the water begins to generate waves in the bathtub. If you think about the power of the movement of the Earth's crust moving back and forth, then you'll understand the power that the ocean water will have during a tsunami.

WHAT HAPPENS DURING A TSUNAMI?

STEP 1: Once water is displaced by an earthquake or other cause, the ocean waves begin to quickly move out from the center of where the movement initially happened.

STEP 2: Depending on the force of the initial event, the waves can speed across the ocean at rates of up to 500 miles per hour. They can continue for thousands of miles.

Isometric representation of natural disaster.

STEP 3: At this point, the crest of the tsunami may not be that tall. In fact, in deep ocean waters, tsunamis may remain unseen because their crests are not that high, perhaps just a few feet above the water.

STEP 4: As the waves head toward the coastline, they begin to pile up on top of each other and their height grows.

STEP 5: As the tsunami approaches, the water actually draws backwards, away from the coastline and it may leave shallow water or beach exposed along the shore. If people are unaware of what is happening, they may find this unusual, and move forward on to the beach instead of running away from the powerful waves that are coming.

STEP 6: Once the wave finally hits the shore, it will be more like a wall of water than a wave. The water will travel over the coastline and move quickly inland at high speed and with enormous power. The height of the tsunami will vary depending on the original event that caused it, as well as the physical features of the coastline. The waves may be 100 feet or more in height.

STEP 7: A tsunami usually isn't just one wave. It's a series of waves with time in between. The series of large waves is a wave train. The first wave isn't always the largest in the series. People who have experienced and lived through a tsunami have said that it sounds like a freight train.

A small boat being captured by a large wave.

WHERE DO TSUNAMIS HAPPEN?

A tsunami can happen wherever a displacement of water occurs in any large body of water. They occur with the most frequency in the Pacific Ocean along the *"Ring Of Fire"* where earthquakes and volcanoes are commonplace. All the countries that border the Pacific Ocean are at risk for tsunamis.

RING   OF   FIRE
Aleutian trench
Kurile trench
Japan trench
Izu Bonin trench
Ryukyu trench
Philippine trench
Marianas trench
Challenger Deep
Bougainville trench
Java (Sunda) trench
Tonga trench
Kermadec trench
Middle America trench
Puerto Rico trench
Peru-Chile trench
South Sandwich trench
Equator

WHY IS A TSUNAMI DANGEROUS?

Tsunamis can travel through the ocean at the rate of 500 miles per hour. They can traverse the entire ocean in less than a day. When they get closer to shore, they slow down. However, they still hit the shore at speeds of 50 miles per hour or more. They can flood up to 1,000 feet inland. The energy generated by a tsunami can flip cars and trucks, destroy buildings, and lift up giant boulders.

Pacific Ring of Fire.

It can also travel up rivers and streams once it hits shore. Tsunamis don't always cause giant waves. Sometimes they appear as a very rapidly rising tide with a lot of underwater turbulence. They can strip entire beaches on the coast. People can be sucked under the tsunami's waves and heavy objects can be tossed around as if they were toys.

Pacific Ring of Fire. White smoky vent fluid rises out of small sulfur chimneys at Northwest Eifuku volcano. This area was named Champagne vent because bubbles of liquid CO_2 were rising out of the seafloor.

TSUNAMI
HAZARD
ZONE

TSUNAMI WARNINGS

Some areas have such frequent earthquakes that tsunamis are a constant threat. The National Oceanic and Atmospheric Administration has created a system that uses buoys in the ocean to detect tsunamis so that people can leave at risk areas in time. This system is called DART for Deep-Ocean Assessment and Reporting of Tsunamis.

Tsunami hazard zone sign.

Surfing the Spray.

COULD YOU SURF ON A TSUNAMI WAVE?

Some people think it would be interesting to surf a tsunami wave, but this isn't possible, even for the most expert surfers. They don't resemble the waves at historic surfing sites such as Maverick's. A tsunami wave is like a wall of water. It doesn't stack up in the same way as a breaking wave does. The wave may be 100 miles long and its tail is traveling at the breakneck speed of about 500 mph. The portion of the wave that hits the shore is very thick.

The surfboard has nowhere to grip because the wave doesn't have a "face." The other factor is that the water is filled with debris, like garbage, materials from buildings, dead animals and people. You can't duck-dive the wave either. That's because the whole column of water is in motion not just the top edge. There's no way to exit as well since the trough is possibly as far as 100 miles away.

Expert Hawaiian surfer Garrett McNamara has ridden a certain type of tsunami wave generated by the fall of glacier ice. He stated afterwards that it was the closest to death he ever came.

Giant tsunami waves, old fortress, tower.

FASCINATING FACTS ABOUT TSUNAMIS

- The tallest tsunami on record happened in Lituya Bay in Alaska in 1958. Its height was a staggering 1,720 feet. It was taller than the Empire State Building.

- In 2004 the Indian Ocean tsunami claimed the lives of over 220,000 people in 14 different countries. It was triggered by a powerful 9.1 magnitude earthquake off the coast of Sumatra in Indonesia. The earthquake that caused the tsunami had the energy of about 23,000 atomic explosions.

- The first recorded tsunami took place in 479 BC. A Persian army was invading the town of Potidaea, Greece when the water receded from the shore followed by a towering wave of water. The historian Herodotus thought the Greek god of the sea Poseidon was angry and had caused the wave.

- If you have the misfortune to be in the water during a tsunami, it's better to grab a floating object and hold on instead of trying to swim.

- Scientists can estimate the time when a tsunami will hit the coastline based on the ocean depth, the distance from the event to the coastline, and the time of the earthquake or other cause.

- Tsunamis can travel all the way across the ocean with a limited loss of their original energy.

- The Hawaiian Islands are always at risk for tsunamis. They get at least one every year and a powerful one every 7 years or so. The biggest one that ever occurred there was in 1946. It hit the island of Hilo with 30-foot tall waves.

- About 3.5 million years ago, an enormous meteor crashed into the ocean. It created a mega tsunami that ripped through the oceans several times.

- Tsunamis are often called tidal waves but they have nothing to do with tides at all.

- In March of 2011, the tsunami generated by Japan's Tohoku earthquake reached a height of about 130 feet. It destroyed coastal towns and caused accidents at nuclear power plants. Over 15,000 people were killed.

- On average two tsunamis occur worldwide every year. Every 15 years or so a very destructive ocean tsunami occurs.

- Do you live in a coastal area along the *"Ring Of Fire"*? If you ever feel a very strong earthquake or hear a loud roaring sound coming from the ocean, it's time to go to higher ground or inland. By the time you see water receding from the coastline, it may be too late.

This is why so many people around the world died in the 2004 Indian Ocean tsunami. They didn't recognize the dangers of the receding water and instead of escaping to higher ground they stayed in the water.

Now you know more about the danger of tsunamis. You can find more books about the environment from Baby Professor by searching the website of your favorite book retailer.

Visit
BABY PROFESSOR
EDUCATION KIDS
www.BabyProfessorBooks.com
to download Free Baby Professor eBooks
and view our catalog of new and exciting
Children's Books